SOUL DETOX

Clean Living in a Contaminated World

Also by Craig Groeschel

Participant's Guide

FIVE SESSIONS

SOUL DETOX

Clean Living in a Contaminated World

CRAIG GROESCHEL

Author of *The Christian Atheist*

with Christine M. Anderson

ZONDERVAN.com/
AUTHORTRACKER
follow your favorite authors

ZONDERVAN

Soul Detox Participant's Guide
Copyright © 2012 by Craig Groeschel

This title is also available as a Zondervan ebook. Visit www.zondervan.com/ebooks.

Requests for information should be addressed to:

Zondervan, *Grand Rapids, Michigan 49530*

ISBN 978-0-310-89492-6

Published in association with Winters, King & Associates, Inc.

Cover design: Curt Diepenhorst
Cover photography: Jeffrey Coolidge / Getty Images®
Interior design: David Conn

Printed in the United States of America

12 13 14 15 16 /DCI/ 20 19 18 17 16 15 14 13 12 11 10 9 8 7 6 5 4 3 2 1

CONTENTS

How to Use This Guide   7

SESSION 1
    Lethal Language   9
    Experiencing the Power of Life-Giving Words

SESSION 2
    Scare Pollution   31
    Unlocking the Chokehold of Fear

SESSION 3
    Radioactive Relationships   45
    Loving Unhealthy People without Getting Sick

SESSION 4
    Septic Thoughts   59
    Overcoming Our False Beliefs

SESSION 5
    Germ Warfare   79
    Cleansing Our Lives of Cultural Toxins

HOW TO USE THIS GUIDE

Group Size

The *Soul Detox* video curriculum is designed to be experienced in a group setting such as a Bible study, Sunday school class, or any small group gathering. To ensure everyone has enough time to participate in discussions, it is recommended that large groups break up into smaller groups of four to six people each.

Materials Needed

Each participant should have his or her own Participant's Guide, which includes video outline notes, directions for activities and discussion questions, as well as personal studies to deepen learning between sessions.

Timing

The time notations — for example (17 minutes) — indicate the *actual* time of video segments and the *suggested* time for each activity or discussion. For example:

Individual Activity: What I Want to Remember (2 Minutes)

Adhering to the suggested times will enable you to complete each session in one hour. If you have a longer meeting, you may wish to allow more time for discussion and activities. You may also opt to devote two meetings rather than one to each session. In addition to allowing discussions to be more spacious, this has the added advantage of allowing group members to read related chapters in the *Soul Detox* book and to complete the personal study between meetings. In the second meeting, devote the time allotted for watching the video to discussing group members' insights and questions from their reading and personal study.

Facilitation

Each group should appoint a facilitator who is responsible for starting the video and for keeping track of time during discussions and activities. Facilitators may also read questions aloud and monitor discussions, prompting participants to respond and assuring that everyone has the opportunity to participate.

Personal Studies

Maximize the impact of the curriculum with additional study between group sessions. Every personal study includes reflection questions, Bible study, and a guided prayer activity. You'll get the most out of the curriculum by setting aside about one hour between sessions for personal study. For each session, you may wish to complete the personal study all in one sitting or to spread it out over a few days.

LETHAL LANGUAGE

Experiencing the Power of Life-Giving Words

The tongue is a thermometer; it gives us our spiritual temperature. It is also a thermostat; it regulates our spiritual temperature. Control of the tongue can mean everything.

RICHARD J. FOSTER, *CELEBRATION OF DISCIPLINE*

Welcome

Welcome to Session 1 of *Soul Detox*. If this is your first time together as a group, take a moment to introduce yourselves to each other before watching the video. Then let's get started!

Video: Lethal Language (12 Minutes)

Play the video segment for Session 1. As you watch, use the outline (below and page 11) to follow along or to take notes on anything that stands out to you.

Notes

"The tongue has the power of life and death" (Proverbs 18:21a).

The Bible contrasts life-giving words and toxic words:

"Reckless words pierce like a sword, but the tongue of the wise brings healing" (Proverbs 12:18 NIV 1984).

"The tongue that brings healing is a tree of life, but a deceitful tongue crushes the spirit" (Proverbs 15:4 NIV 1984).

We must guard our hearts against toxic words (see Proverbs 4:23).

Truth vs. trash: When people speak words about you, is what they say true? If so, believe it and embrace it. If it's trash, reject it.

Every chance you get, speak life-giving words.

> "Do not let any unwholesome talk come out of your mouths, but only what is helpful for building others up" (Ephesians 4:29a).

Any time you think something positive, say it. Why rob someone of a blessing by keeping a positive statement to yourself?

Don't internalize the toxic words that others speak about you. Guard your heart.

Group Discussion (46 Minutes)

Take a few minutes to talk about what you just watched.

1. What part of the teaching had the most impact on you?

Toxic Words

2. A toxic substance is something that causes serious harm or even death. *Toxikon*, the Greek origin of the English word "toxic," refers to an archer's bow armed with a poison arrow. The psalmist uses this very image to describe the power of toxic words:

> [Evildoers] sharpen their tongues like swords and aim cruel words like deadly arrows (Psalm 64:3).

The author of Proverbs draws on a similar image:

The words of the reckless pierce like swords (Proverbs 12:18a).

- Those who speak toxic words in these verses are "evildoers" and "the reckless." How would you describe the similarities and differences in how words are used by someone who is an evildoer and someone who is reckless? If you can think of any, use examples — from the news, social media, books, movies, etc. — to describe both.

- Overall, how would you characterize the people whose words have wounded you? As evildoers, as reckless, or as something else?

- At some point in our lives, all of us have spoken words that wound. What thoughts or feelings are you aware of when you consider how the words *evildoer* and *reckless* might characterize you?

Guard Your Heart

3. Toxic words are words that lodge in the heart and cause deep wounds. When we internalize these words, we allow them to distort the truth about who we are — and that impacts everything. The Bible's familiar wisdom about this comes from Proverbs:

    Above all else, guard your heart, for everything you do flows from it (Proverbs 4:23).

In ancient Hebrew thought, the heart referred to more than just the center of emotions. It included the "entire inner life of a person"[1] — everything we might describe as psychological, spiritual, intellectual, and emotional. To guard your heart, then, is to guard the essence of who God created you to be.

- What examples come to mind when you think of what it means in practical terms to guard your heart? How have you done this well, or how have you witnessed someone you know doing this well?

- How would you describe the differences between guarding your heart and being overly self-protective in your relationships?

4. The verses that follow Proverbs 4:23 elaborate on it by listing specific behaviors that guard the heart:

> Keep your mouth free of perversity; keep corrupt talk far from your lips. Let your eyes look straight ahead; fix your gaze directly before you. Give careful thought to the paths for your feet and be steadfast in all your ways. Do not turn to the right or the left; keep your foot from evil (Proverbs 4:24 – 27).

The first behavior on the list — the one the Proverbs writer perhaps considers most important — directly addresses the power of words. It's easy to recognize the impact of toxic words spoken to us by someone else, but this passage emphasizes the need to guard our hearts from *our own words*.

Take a moment to recall a recent or past occasion when you were careless or misleading with your words. For example, you said something unkind, had an angry outburst, or spun the truth

---

1. Alex Luc, "(*leb, lebab*) heart," *New International Dictionary of Old Testament Theology and Exegesis*, vol. 2, Willem A. VanGemeren, gen. ed. (Grand Rapids: Zondervan, 1997), 749.

to make yourself look better. How might you have internalized what you said? In other words, how might your careless or misleading words have harmed your heart by distorting the truth of who you are?

Life-Giving Words

5. The Bible uses vivid images to describe the impact of life-giving words:

> The soothing tongue is a tree of life (Proverbs 15:4a).
>
> Gracious words are a honeycomb, sweet to the soul and healing to the bones (Proverbs 16:24).
>
> The right word at the right time is like precious gold set in silver (Proverbs 25:11 CEV).

- Which image resonates most with your own experience of life-giving words? Why?

- In the last day or two, what experiences, if any, have you had of giving or receiving life-giving words? How would you describe the impact these words had — on you and on the other person?

- Some words are not only life-giving but life-changing. Have you, or has someone you know, experienced life-changing words? Briefly share the situation, the life-changing words, and what happened as a result.

6. The four remaining sessions in *Soul Detox* explore the potentially toxic impact of fear, unhealthy people, false beliefs, and popular culture. These are important topics to be sure, but perhaps even more important are the ways you'll experience God at work among you — especially in how you relate to each other and share your lives throughout the study. As you discuss the teaching in each session, there will be many opportunities to practice giving and receiving life-giving, heart-guarding, and truth-telling words.

Take a few moments to consider the kinds of words and conversations that are important to you in this setting. What do you need or want to hear from the other members of the group? Use one or more of the sentence starters below, or your own statement, to help the group understand the best way to speak life and truth to you. As each person responds, use the chart on pages 16 – 17 to briefly note what is important to that person and how you can companion them well.

It really helps me when ...

I tend to withdraw when ...

I'll know this group is a safe place if you ...

In our discussions, the best thing you could do for me is ...

NAME	THE BEST WAY I CAN COMPANION THIS PERSON IS ...
Kelley	It a safe place if she wants to confess something.
Stephanie	It really helps me when I have accountability.
Wally	It really helps me when I have accountability
Bill	It helps when someone counts on you as a brother in Christ.
Kreg	The best thing you could do for me is pray & encourage.

NAME	THE BEST WAY I CAN COMPANION THIS PERSON IS ...
Heather	I'll know this group is a safe place when you know I have a seewed veiew of the world.

Individual Activity: What I Want to Remember (2 Minutes)

Complete this activity on your own.

1. Briefly review the outline and any notes you took.
2. In the space below, write down the most significant thing you gained in this session — from the teaching, activities, or discussions.

   What I want to remember from this session ...

Closing Prayer

Close your time together with prayer.

Personal Study

● Read and Learn

Read chapter 3 of the *Soul Detox* book. Use the space below to note any insights or questions you want to bring to the next group session.

● Study and Reflect

When someone says something to or about you, train yourself to categorize the words [as] Truth or Trash. Analyze the message and source before swallowing and digesting what someone else wants to feed you. Are their words true? Based in Scripture? Supported by data over time? If so, embrace them. Allow those life-giving words to minister to your soul and conform you to the image of Christ. If their words are untrue, mean-spirited, and critical without being constructive, then call them what they are— toxic waste. Reject those words. Don't let them into your soul. Take out the trash and leave it by the curb. Delete toxic words and insert the truth.

Soul Detox, page 60

---

1. Toxic words are words that wound and distort the truth of who God created you to be. Which of the significant relationships listed below have been sources of toxic words in your life? Check all that apply.

☐ Parent, guardian, or other childhood caregiver

☐ Grandparent

☐ Sibling

☐ Son or daughter

☐ Extended family member

☐ Spouse, fiancé(e), or other romantic relationship

☐ Teacher, coach, or other student leader

☐ Friend

☐ Pastor or other spiritual leader

☐ Boss or supervisor

☐ Work colleague

☐ Neighbor

☐ Other:

Briefly review the relationships you checked. Which ones stand out most to you? For example, perhaps you recall their words most vividly, they continue to harm you with their words, or what they said had long-term consequences. Of the relationships you checked, circle up to three that stand out most to you.

In the left column of the chart below, write down the toxic statements these people have made. You could write one statement for each relationship you circled or multiple statements made by one person. Use the right column to briefly describe the impact these words had on you.

TOXIC WORDS	THE IMPACT THESE WORDS HAD ON ME

When you guard your heart from toxic words, you filter what others say to you or about you to distinguish truth from trash. Keeping in mind the toxic words you wrote down and the impact they had on you, read through the twelve truths on pages 22 – 23. Place a checkmark next to any truths that catch your attention.

Using the truths you checked as a filter, what distortions or lies can you identify in what you wrote on your chart?

How do the truths themselves impact you? For example, do you find it difficult to embrace them as truths that apply to you personally? Resonate with them deeply? Believe them more with your head than with your heart?

What do you need from God, or how do you want God to help you in connection with the toxic words that have impacted you?

TWELVE TRUTHS

✔	TRUTH	SCRIPTURE
	I am a child of God.	But to all who believed him and accepted him, he gave the right to become children of God (John 1:12 NLT). God decided in advance to adopt us into his own family by bringing us to himself through Jesus Christ (Ephesians 1:5a NLT).
	I am loved by God.	Even before he made the world, God loved us and chose us (Ephesians 1:4a NLT). But because of his great love for us, God, who is rich in mercy, made us alive with Christ (Ephesians 2:4–5a).
	I am free and forgiven.	He is so rich in kindness and grace that he purchased our freedom with the blood of his Son and forgave our sins (Ephesians 1:7 NLT). So now there is no condemnation for those who belong to Christ Jesus (Romans 8:1 NLT).
	My body belongs to God.	Don't you realize that your body is the temple of the Holy Spirit, who lives in you and was given to you by God? You do not belong to yourself, for God bought you with a high price (1 Corinthians 6:19–20a NLT).
	God is close to me.	The Lord is near to all who call on him, to all who call on him in truth (Psalm 145:18). Once you were far away from God, but now you have been brought near to him through the blood of Christ (Ephesians 2:13b NLT).
	I am attractive/ beautiful from the inside out.	You should clothe yourselves instead with the beauty that comes from within, the unfading beauty of a gentle and quiet spirit, which is so precious to God (1 Peter 3:4 NLT). People judge by outward appearance, but the Lord looks at the heart (1 Samuel 16:7b NLT).

✔	TRUTH	SCRIPTURE
	God will never abandon me.	The Lord has promised that he will not leave us or desert us (Hebrews 13:5b CEV). So do not fear, for I am with you; do not be dismayed, for I am your God (Isaiah 41:10a).
	I am gifted by God. I can accomplish great things.	A spiritual gift is given to each of us so we can help each other (1 Corinthians 12:7 NLT). Very truly I tell you, whoever believes in me will do the works I have been doing, and they will do even greater things than these, because I am going to the Father (John 14:12).
	God cares about me and my problems.	Give all your worries and cares to God, for he cares about you (1 Peter 5:7 NLT). For [God] will deliver the needy who cry out, the afflicted who have no one to help (Psalm 72:12).
	God gives me strength and protection.	The Lord is faithful, and he will strengthen you and protect you from the evil one (2 Thessalonians 3:3). For he will command his angels concerning you to guard you in all your ways (Psalm 91:11).
	I have a future.	"For I know the plans I have for you," declares the Lord, "plans to prosper you and not to harm you, plans to give you hope and a future" (Jeremiah 29:11). Forgetting the past and looking forward to what lies ahead, I press on to reach the end of the race and receive the heavenly prize for which God, through Christ Jesus, is calling us (Philippians 3:13b–14 NLT).
	With God's help, I can change.	And the Lord—who is the Spirit—makes us more and more like him as we are changed into his glorious image (2 Corinthians 3:18b NLT). I will give you a new heart, and I will put a new spirit in you. I will take out your stony, stubborn heart and give you a tender, responsive heart (Ezekiel 36:26 NLT).

2. Toxic words are always painful, but not all painful words are toxic. Sometimes it's the truthful words that hurt the most. And the Bible encourages us to welcome the wounds that come from these words:

> Wounds from a sincere friend are better than many kisses from an enemy (Proverbs 27:6 NLT).

> Let the godly strike me! It will be a kindness! If they correct me, it is soothing medicine. Don't let me refuse it (Psalm 141:5a NLT).

Consider these passages first from the perspective of the person who *speaks* a wounding truth, and then from the perspective of the person who *receives* a wounding truth. What thoughts or feelings arise when you consider the prospect of both speaking and receiving a painful truth?

Both verses describe qualifications for the one who delivers a wounding truth: the person must be a "sincere friend" and "godly." "Speaking the truth in love" is also an essential requirement for Christ followers (Ephesians 4:15a). When you reflect on your significant relationships, how would you characterize the degree to which you and the other people in your life either meet these qualifications or are intentional about trying to do so?

We tend to avoid or actively resist things that cause us pain, but is there anything about the practice of giving and receiving difficult truths that intrigues you or stirs up hope in you for your own relationships? What good things would you hope to gain if giving and receiving truth were a normal part of your relationships?

Your words matter. They are either giving life or taking life. Choose to give life.
Soul Detox, page 62

---

3. We can avoid the most obvious verbal sins and still "take life" with how we use, or fail to use, our words. Take a moment to recall some of your conversations over the last day or two and then review the following list. Place a check next to any behaviors you engaged in during your recent conversations.

☐ Exaggerating
☐ Impression management (spinning the truth to make yourself look better)
☐ Talking too much
☐ Yelling
☐ Cursing
☐ Bragging
☐ Complaining
☐ Saying something false or damaging about someone
☐ Being critical or judgmental
☐ Trying to say something smart, funny, or spiritual to impress someone

- ☐ Withholding truth or other important information
- ☐ Using phrases like "You *always*" or "You *never*"
- ☐ Gossiping
- ☐ Interrupting
- ☐ Belittling or diminishing someone else's experiences or views
- ☐ Keeping a conversation focused on others as a way to avoid revealing anything about yourself
- ☐ Denying authentic emotion (for example, saying you're not angry when you are angry)
- ☐ Being harsh rather than loving with truth
- ☐ Dominating a conversation
- ☐ Retaliating
- ☐ Flattery or sweet talk (using compliments to earn favor or get something you want)
- ☐ Self-justifying
- ☐ Refusing to apologize or acknowledge a fault
- ☐ Using humor or sarcasm to zing someone else or to avoid being vulnerable
- ☐ Other:

Now take a moment to consider how your conversations over the last day or two have brought life to your relationships. From the following list, place a check next to any life-giving ways you used words during your recent conversations.

- ☐ Celebrating others' accomplishments
- ☐ Praising good behavior or good work
- ☐ Withholding an unnecessary comment
- ☐ Extending grace instead of judgment
- ☐ Offering forgiveness or an apology
- ☐ Speaking words of comfort or encouragement
- ☐ Saying thank you
- ☐ Withholding a complaint
- ☐ Asking "How are you?" and really wanting to hear the answer
- ☐ Speaking the truth in love
- ☐ Listening without calculating how to switch the focus of the conversation back to you

☐ Expressing your belief in someone
☐ Practicing simplicity in speech (what the Bible describes as letting your yes be yes and your no be no)
☐ Refraining from gossip or idle chatter
☐ Blessing rather than cursing someone who hurt you
☐ Praying for someone
☐ Pausing to consider your reply before giving it
☐ Saying, "Tell me more about that."
☐ Being graciously honest about your thoughts or feelings (not engaging in people-pleasing by withholding your opinion or denying anger or hurt)
☐ Expressing contentment or gratitude for the good things in your life

Compare what you checked on both lists (pages 25–27). What do you notice? For example, is there a significant difference in the number of things you checked on each list? If so, why? What similarities or differences are there between the kinds of people or situations that prompt you to use life-taking words and those that lead you to use life-giving words?

4. Like us, the psalmist also struggled with controlling his words, and sought God's help to use them well:

> Take control of what I say, O LORD, and guard my lips. Don't let me drift toward evil or take part in acts of wickedness (Psalm 141:3 – 4a NLT).

> Let my words and my thoughts be pleasing to you, LORD, because you are my mighty rock and my protector (Psalm 19:14 CEV).

Briefly review the items you checked in response to the first list for question 3 (pages 25–26). How would you describe your greatest weaknesses or the ways in which your words tend to "drift toward evil"?

Now review the items you checked in response to the second list for question 3 (pages 26–27). How would you describe your greatest strengths or the ways in which your words are routinely pleasing to God?

● Guided Prayer

God, your words have changed my life. Thank you for all the ways you communicate your love and care for me.

I need your help with some toxic words that have hurt me. Please show me how I can let go of the trash and hold onto the truth with this situation ...

I also want my relationships to be characterized by truth, but painful truths are hard for me. Prepare my heart to give and receive hard truths, especially in my relationship(s) with ...

Forgive me for the life-taking words I have spoken recently ...

Lord, guard my lips and keep me from being reckless with what I say. I want all of my words to give life and be pleasing to you — this day and every day. Amen.

Aunt Kay
Men's retreat
Men + Women Weekend
Stephanie traveling
Jeni + family

- Men + Women of 37 + 38

SCARE POLLUTION

Unlocking the Chokehold of Fear

$1.50 Per burger
$3.⁰⁰ w/chips + drink > *10:30 - 2:00*

We are inwardly constructed in nerve and tissue, brain
cell and soul, for faith and not for fear. God made us
that way. To live by worry is to live against reality.

E. STANLEY JONES, TRANSFORMED BY THORNS

Oct. 13ᵗʰ Possible bake sale/donuts
for Megan Hoel fundraiser
rummage.

Group Discussion: Checking In (5 Minutes)

Welcome to Session 2 of *Soul Detox*. A key part of getting to know God better is sharing your journey with others. Before watching the video, briefly check in with each other about your experiences since the last session. For example:

- What insights did you discover in the personal study or in the chapter you read from the *Soul Detox* book?
- How did the last session impact your daily life or your relationship with God?
- What questions would you like to ask the other members of your group?

Video: Scare Pollution (11 Minutes)

Play the video segment for Session 2. As you watch, use the outline (below and page 33) to follow along or to take notes on anything that stands out to you.

Notes

Four common fears

1. Fear of loss *Spouse*
   Kids
   Financial

2. Fear of failure

3. Fear of rejection

4. Fear of the unknown

"For God has not given us a spirit of fear, but of power and of love and of a sound mind" (2 Timothy 1:7 NKJV).

Fear is having faith; it's just placing your faith in the wrong things.

With God's help, we can overcome our spirit of fear.

Definition of fear: placing our faith in the what-ifs.

What we fear really matters.

What you fear reveals what you value the most.

What you fear reveals where you trust God the least.

He can't bless us if we don't trust him.

"I sought the LORD, and he answered me; he delivered me from all my fears" (Psalm 34:4).

When you acknowledge where you trust God the least and you seek him, he will deliver you from your fears.

Group Discussion (42 Minutes)

Take a few minutes to talk about what you just watched.

1. What part of the teaching had the most impact on you?

What You Fear

2. Briefly describe one of your most intense or prolonged experiences of fear. How did the fear impact you? Consider the following areas:

   - *Physical*: for example, shortness of breath, tears, hyper-alertness, rapid heartbeat, sweating, fatigue, etc.

   - *Emotional*: for example, terror, numbness, depression, grief, loss of hope, etc.

   - *Mental*: for example, significantly increased or decreased ability to focus or make decisions, runaway thoughts, irrationality, etc.

   - *Relational*: for example, deeper dependence on others, inability to connect, withdrawal, increased willingness to ask for help, etc.

   - *Spiritual*: for example, significantly increased or diminished awareness of God's presence, feeling abandoned, questioning the existence or goodness of God, complete surrender to God's care, etc.

3. On the video, Craig named four common fears: *loss, failure, rejection, the unknown.*

   - Of the four, which kind of fear would you say you relate to most?

   - Briefly describe a recent experience of that kind of fear or how you tend to behave because of that fear. For example, "Last week, my boss announced that there might be layoffs this year. Now I can't sleep at night because I'm afraid I might lose my job." Or, "I tend to avoid setting goals because I'm afraid of setting myself up to fail."

What You Value and Trust

4. To have faith is to believe in something or to trust someone. Craig defined fear as placing our faith — our beliefs and our trust — not in God but in the "what-ifs." *What if ... I don't get better? We lose the house? She doesn't love me? I fail the exam? God doesn't come through for me this time?*

   Below and on the next page are several examples of fear from the Bible. Go around the group and have a different person read each passage aloud. As the passages are read, underline any words or phrases that stand out to you. You may wish to read through the list twice to give everyone time to listen and respond.

   When the men of that place asked [Isaac] about his wife, he said, "She is my sister," because he was afraid to say, "She is my wife." He thought, "The men of this place might kill me on account of Rebekah, because she is beautiful" (Genesis 26:7).

   The man said, "Who made you ruler and judge over us? Are you thinking of killing me as you killed the Egyptian?" Then Moses was afraid and thought, "What I did must have become known" (Exodus 2:14).

Then Peter got down out of the boat, walked on the water and came toward Jesus. But when he saw the wind, he was afraid and, beginning to sink, cried out, "Lord, save me!" (Matthew 14:29–30).

Yet at the same time many even among the leaders believed in [Jesus]. But because of the Pharisees they would not openly acknowledge their faith for fear they would be put out of the synagogue; for they loved human praise more than praise from God (John 12:42–43).

- If fear is placing trust in the what-ifs, how would you describe the different what-ifs that made Isaac, Moses, Peter, and the leaders afraid?

Real

- What would you say each person valued most? Where did each person trust God the least?

5. Take a moment to consider one of your own what-ifs (perhaps connected to the fear you mentioned in response to question 2).

- Make an "I believe" or an "I trust" statement based on this fear. For example, if you are afraid of losing your job, your belief statement might be, "I believe my job is the source of my security." If you fear the unknown, you might make a statement like, "I trust in my ability to control what happens to me." If you are afraid of rejection, you might say, "I believe no one else will love me."

- What might your statement reveal about what you value most and where you trust God the least?

Delivered from Fear

6. When we are afraid, God promises to help us — not just with the threatening situation but also with the fear itself. The psalmist testifies to his own experience of God's deliverance:

> I sought the LORD, and he answered me; he delivered me from all my fears (Psalm 34:4).

The Hebrew word for "sought" is *daras* (daw-rash´). Depending on the usage, *daras* may also be translated as *care about, consult, inquire, study, investigate*. It is an active verb and conveys the focus and determination of the one who seeks. Elsewhere, the psalmist describes the wise as those who *daras* God (Psalm 53:2), and the wicked as those who are too proud to *daras* God (Psalm 10:4).[2]

The Hebrew word for "delivered" is *nasal* (naw-tsal´). *Nasal* may also be translated as *rescued, saved, snatched away, pulled out, extricated*. It evokes the image of being freed from a dangerous trap. In addition to deliverance from fear, the psalmist also affirms God's ability to rescue (*nasal*) his people from such threats as enemies (Psalm 31:15), evildoers (Psalm 59:2), troubles (Psalm 54:7), and distress (Psalm 107:6).[3]

---

1. David Denninger, "(*drš*) seek," *New International Dictionary of Old Testament Theology and Exegesis*, vol. 1, Willem A. VanGemeren, gen. ed. (Grand Rapids: Zondervan, 1997), 993–995.

2. Robert L. Hubbard, Jr., "(*nṣl*) rescue," *New International Dictionary of Old Testament Theology and Exegesis*, vol. 3, Willem A. VanGemeren, gen. ed. (Grand Rapids: Zondervan, 1997), 141, 144.

- Psalm 34:4 describes both human and divine activity: the psalmist *seeks* God, and God *answers* and *delivers*. Using the descriptions of *daras* and *nasal* as a reference, how would you describe the human and divine activity related to a fear you're facing now? In other words, what behaviors or activities does your fear prompt in you? How do you recognize — or struggle to recognize — God's response to your activity?

- How do you imagine your life would be different if God delivered you from this fear?

7. At the end of the group discussion for Session 1, you had the opportunity to share with the group how you'd like them to speak life and truth to you, and to write down the best ways you can companion the other members of the group (see chart on pages 16 – 17).

    - Briefly restate what you asked for from the group in Session 1. What changes or clarifications would you like to make that would help the group know more about how to companion you well? As each person responds, add any additional information to the chart. (If you were absent from the last session, share your response to question 6 on page 15. Then use the chart to write down what is important to each member of the group.)

- In what ways, if any, did you find yourself responding differently to other members of the group in this session based on what they asked for in the previous session? What made that easy or difficult for you to do?

Individual Activity: What I Want to Remember (2 Minutes)

Complete this activity on your own.

1. Briefly review the outline and any notes you took.
2. In the space below, write down the most significant thing you gained in this session — from the teaching, activities, or discussions.

What I want to remember from this session …

Closing Prayer

Close your time together with prayer.

Personal Study

● Read and Learn

Read chapter 8 of the *Soul Detox* book. Use the space below to note any insights or questions you want to bring to the next group session.

● Study and Reflect

Admit what you're afraid of. Identify it clearly. Until you do, it will continue to be that elephant in the room, that huge dark cloud hovering over you that you're not willing to talk about. So do some name calling. Check the label and see the brand of fear you're wearing.

Soul Detox, page 150

1. On the DVD, Craig identified four common fears most of us struggle with at some point: fear of loss, fear of failure, fear of rejection, and fear of the unknown. What fears — small or large — are you aware of in each of these areas?

   Fear of loss

   Fear of failure

   Fear of rejection

   Fear of the unknown

Of the four kinds of fear, which would you say is your "brand" — the kind of fear you struggle with most? Circle that kind of fear and keep it in mind for the remainder of the study.

God has not given you a spirit of fear. If you're feeling afraid, that's not from him. Don't accept it. Don't give in to it. What God has given you is a spirit of power, of love, and a sound mind. Seek him. Fear not, for the Lord is with you.

Soul Detox, page 155

---

2. The phrase "Do not be afraid" (or "Do not fear") is among the most common — and perhaps most neglected — of biblical commands. Almost always, it is spoken directly by God or Jesus, or by a prophet or divine messenger who speaks on God's behalf.

Following are three do-not-be-afraid statements from the New Testament. Read through them slowly, paying particular attention to how God is at work.

An angel of the Lord appeared to [Joseph] in a dream and said, "Joseph son of David, do not be afraid to take Mary home as your wife, because what is conceived in her is from the Holy Spirit" (Matthew 1:20).

[Appearing to the disciples after the resurrection] Jesus said to them, "Do not be afraid. Go and tell my brothers to go to Galilee; there they will see me" (Matthew 28:10).

One night the Lord spoke to Paul in a vision: "Do not be afraid; keep on speaking, do not be silent. For I am with you, and no one is going to attack and harm you, because I have many people in this city" (Acts 18:9 – 10).

It is interesting to note that what all three people feared was a direct result of God's presence or activity in their lives. They were afraid, at least initially, because they didn't recognize God at work in what was happening to them.

When you consider the fears you identified in question 1, do you think something like this might be true for you as well? In what ways might the things you fear be the result of God's presence or activity in your life?

Our natural response is to distance ourselves from the things we're afraid of. In the case of Joseph, the disciples, and the apostle Paul, running from their fears would have meant running from God. Instead, they responded to God's do-not-be-afraid command and kept moving toward what initially frightened them.

What thoughts or emotions are you aware of when you consider the possibility of moving toward your fears rather than running from them?

Start seeking God, and don't stop. When you diligently, consistently, tirelessly seek him, your fears will evaporate.... Start in his Word. Call out to him in prayer. Seek him with your friends who also follow Christ. Ask them to pray for you. Ask them to pray that God will reveal himself to you, and that he'll show you the path to overcoming your fears. Don't stop.

Soul Detox, **pages 153–154**

---

3. When we are afraid, choosing to seek God is an act of trust — a trust based on who God is and our belief that his promises are true. Scripture is rich with God's promises for those who seek him. With your own fears in mind, read through the following promises and underline any words or phrases that stand out to you.

The LORD is good to those whose hope is in him, to the one who seeks him; it is good to wait quietly for the salvation of the LORD (Lamentations 3:25 – 26).

When you call on me, when you come and pray to me, I'll listen. When you come looking for me, you'll find me. Yes, when you get serious about finding me and want it more than anything else, I'll make sure you won't be disappointed (Jeremiah 29:12 – 13 MSG).

Trust in the LORD with all your heart; do not depend on your own understanding. Seek his will in all you do, and he will show you which path to take (Proverbs 3:5 – 6 NLT).

It's impossible to please God apart from faith. And why? Because anyone who wants to approach God must believe both that he exists and that he cares enough to respond to those who seek him (Hebrews 11:6 MSG).

The verse from Lamentations uses three verbs to describe what God wants us to do: *hope*, *seek*, and *wait*. How would you describe the significance of the word order — that first we hope, then seek, and then wait?

How do you sense God might be inviting you to hope, seek, and wait for him in connection with your own fears?

Which of the verses stood out most to you? How does it relate to your own fears or what you most need from God in order to seek him?

● Guided Prayer

God, you are my strong fortress and my deliverer. Thank you for all the ways — seen and unseen — that you provide for me and protect me.
Sometimes I think what I really need protection from is myself. When I am afraid, my mind runs wild imagining all kinds of worst-case scenarios. Please guard my mind, especially my thoughts about ...

Open my eyes and help me to recognize your presence and activity in the things I am afraid of. Help me to trust that you are at work in this situation ...

Give me courage to move toward my fears rather than running away from them. I sense that you may be inviting me to ... In order to move forward, I need ...

Ignite my hope and help me to seek you with my whole heart. Teach me to rest and then to wait quietly in the knowledge that you care about what happens to me and have promised to deliver me from all my fears. Amen.

RADIOACTIVE RELATIONSHIPS

Loving Unhealthy People without Getting Sick

A boundary is simply a property line. It clarifies where you end and the other person begins.... Boundaries help you to be clear about what you are for and against and what you will and won't tolerate in your relationships.

JOHN TOWNSEND, *BEYOND BOUNDARIES*

Group Discussion: Checking In (5 Minutes)

Welcome to Session 3 of *Soul Detox*. A key part of getting to know God better is sharing your journey with others. Before watching the video, briefly check in with each other about your experiences since the last session. For example:

- What insights did you discover in the personal study or in the chapter you read from the *Soul Detox* book?
- How did the last session impact your daily life or your relationship with God?
- What questions would you like to ask the other members of your group?

Video: Radioactive Relationships (12 Minutes)

Play the video segment for Session 3. As you watch, use the outline (below and page 47) to follow along or to take notes on anything that stands out to you.

Notes

The right people build you up and lead you toward Christ; the wrong people can be very toxic.

"Do not be misled: 'Bad company corrupts good character'" (1 Corinthians 15:33).

Three categories of toxic people

   1. Critics (negative)

2. Controllers

3. Tempters

Jesus loved everyone equally, but he didn't treat everyone equally. He created boundaries.

As we grow closer to Christ, we need to create healthy boundaries in relationships that are toxic or could hurt us.

When people don't respect your boundaries, you may need to cut off the relationship — at least for a period of time.

We need to separate ourselves from toxic relationships so we can be spiritually strong and full of God's love.

Sebrina
Bob
Megan

Group Discussion (39 Minutes)

Take a few minutes to talk about what you just watched.

1. What part of the teaching had the most impact on you?

Toxic People

2. On the DVD, Craig described three kinds of toxic people:

   Critics: chronically negative people who find fault in everything

   Controllers: overbearing people who manipulate or force their will on others

   Tempters: persuasive people who encourage you to do things you know you shouldn't

   • Which of the three kinds of toxic people do you find most difficult to deal with?

   • Even if we aren't actively toxic in our relationships, all of us have the capacity for toxic behavior. If you were to ask the people who know you best to describe your toxic tendency, which of the three categories do you think they might choose? What examples might they cite as evidence of your tendency?

Myron
Megan

3. Which number on the continuum below best describes how you feel when you have a toxic person in your life? Briefly share an experience that illustrates your response.

1	2	3	4	5	6	7	8	9	10

I feel like the toxic person is in control. I can't change his/her behavior and I am miserable and powerless to do anything about it.

I feel like I am in control. I can't change the other person's behavior, but I can take ownership and responsibility for how I feel and respond.

Healthy Boundaries

4. The biblical foundation for healthy boundaries includes the principle of good stewardship. Stewardship applies to financial and material resources, but it also requires taking ownership and responsibility for our lives as a whole: how we use our gifts (1 Peter 4:10), pursue our growth (Hebrews 6:1), care for our bodies (1 Corinthians 16:19 – 20), guard our interior lives (Proverbs 4:23), and conduct our relationships (Galatians 5:14 – 15). As Christ followers, we are stewards of everything God has entrusted to us.

- Based on your experience of toxic relationships, how would you describe the impact these relationships have on your ability to steward your life and your energies well?

- Healthy boundary statements set a limit. For example:

   I'm not participating.

   I'm not going there with you.

   If the conversation goes toward complaining, trash talk, or gossip, I need to step away.

   The next time you try to get me to do something I don't want to do, I'll leave the room.

   That activity is not good for me. I need to take a pass.

What is your comfort level with setting clear boundaries or with making statements like those on page 49?

• Briefly describe someone you know who has healthy boundaries. How have you seen this person establish or maintain his or her boundaries well? Would you say people tend to respect or resist this person's boundaries? Why?

Managing Toxic Relationships

5. Jesus regularly set boundaries. He loved everyone equally, but he didn't treat everyone equally. And he kept his distance from people who weren't good for him — even those who believed in him. Here is one example:

> In Jerusalem during Passover many people put their faith in Jesus, because they saw him work miracles. But Jesus knew what was in their hearts, and he would not let them have power over him (John 2:23 – 24 CEV).

Other Bible versions describe the boundary Jesus set by saying he "didn't trust them" or "didn't entrust his life to them."

Jesus also had no hesitation in setting vividly clear boundaries with those he was closest to.

> Jesus turned and said to Peter, "Get behind me, Satan! You are a stumbling block to me; you do not have in mind the concerns of God, but merely human concerns" (Matthew 16:23).

• How would you describe the similarities and differences in how Jesus establishes his boundaries in both cases?

- We know Jesus routinely kept his distance from hardhearted and corrupt religious leaders, but in both examples here, he puts a protective fence between himself and his own followers. What unique challenges do you face in establishing boundaries with other Christians? How is it more or less difficult for you than establishing boundaries with non-Christians?

- What connections might you make between Jesus' actions and the principle of good stewardship? In other words, how did he take ownership and responsibility for his life and what God had entrusted to him?

6. Take a few moments to reflect on what you've learned and experienced together in *Soul Detox* so far.

   - Since the first session, what shifts have you noticed in yourself in terms of how you relate to the group? For example, do you feel more or less guarded, understood, challenged, encouraged, connected, etc.?

   - What adjustments, if any, would you like the other group members to make on the Session 1 chart (pages 16 – 17) to help them better companion you?

Individual Activity: What I Want to Remember (2 Minutes)

1. Briefly review the outline and any notes you took.

2. In the space below, write down the most significant thing you gained in this session — from the teaching, activities, or discussions.

What I want to remember from this session ...

Closing Prayer

Close your time together with prayer.

Personal Study

● Read and Learn

Read chapter 11 of the *Soul Detox* book. Use the space below to note any insights or questions you want to bring to the next group session.

● Study and Reflect

The people closest to you will hands down be your greatest spiritual asset or your worst spiritual curse. Those you spend the most time with can propel you closer to God, serving him faithfully and pleasing him in all you do. Or toxic tag-alongs can corrupt your good intentions and rob you of the blessings God wants to pour out on you.

Soul Detox, page 196

---

1. Identify four to six people who are closest to you or with whom you spend the most time in a typical week. Write their names on the lines provided below and on page 54.

☐ _____

☐ _____

☐ _____

☐ _____

☐ _____

☐ _____

Next, consider the impact each person has on you spiritually. Using the scale below, briefly assess the degree to which each relationship may be a spiritual asset or a spiritual liability. Then write the appropriate number in the box next to each person's name on pages 53–54.

+2 =	***Strong spiritual asset***. This person consistently encourages me, brings me joy, speaks truth to me, helps me, or draws me closer to Christ.
+1 =	***Moderate spiritual asset***. This person occasionally encourages me, brings me joy, speaks truth to me, helps me, or draws me closer to Christ.
0 =	***Neither a spiritual asset nor a spiritual liability***.
−1 =	***Moderate spiritual liability***. This person occasionally makes my life difficult, discourages me, manipulates me, hurts me, tempts me, lies to me, or belittles my faith.
−2 =	***Strong spiritual liability***. This person consistently makes my life difficult, discourages me, manipulates me, hurts me, tempts me, lies to me, or belittles my faith.

If applicable, circle the name of one person you assessed as a spiritual liability. If you rated all of your relationships +1 or +2, you are exceedingly blessed! For the remainder of this Personal Study, you may wish to focus instead on any relationship that is challenging for you in some way but fails to rise to the level of being fully toxic.

What specific attitudes or behaviors make this person especially difficult for you to be with?

How do this person's attitudes and behavior impact you — emotionally and spiritually?

[Spiritual gangrene is] what our souls will suffer if we aren't careful about our relationships.... Bad company is toxic to your soul. The wrong relationships corrupt, pollute, infect, rot, and destroy good character.

Soul Detox, page 198

---

2. "A boundary is simply a property line," writes Christian author and psychologist John Townsend. "[It helps] you to be clear about what you are for and against and what you will and won't tolerate in your relationships."

Following are four examples from the Bible that demonstrate different kinds of boundaries. As you read through the passages, pay particular attention to how each one describes what will and won't be tolerated in relationships. Underline any words or phrases that stand out to you.

> I do not sit with the deceitful, nor do I associate with hypocrites. I abhor the assembly of evildoers and refuse to sit with the wicked (Psalm 26:4 – 5).

> I will lead a life of integrity in my own home. I will refuse to look at anything vile and vulgar. I hate all who deal crookedly; I will have nothing to do with them. I will reject perverse ideas and stay away from every evil. I will not tolerate people who slander their neighbors. I will not endure conceit and pride. I will search for faithful people to be my companions (Psalm 101:2b – 6a NLT).

A gossip betrays a confidence; so avoid anyone who talks too much (Proverbs 20:19).

Jesus turned and said to Peter, "Get behind me, Satan! You are a stumbling block to me; you do not have in mind the concerns of God, but merely human concerns" (Matthew 16:23).

What stands out most to you about these boundaries?

Using these passages as a model, what personal boundaries would you make based on the attitudes and behaviors you identified at the end of question 1 (page 55)? In other words, based on what you've experienced in that particular relationship, what is it that you are for and against in any of your relationships? What will you tolerate and not tolerate in any of your relationships?

You have to be willing to set up boundaries so you can be stronger and better minister to people.... Set your standards. Express your standards. Then stand strong. It may seem difficult at first, but the more you practice, the more comfortable you'll become.

Soul Detox, pages 202–203

---

3. Once you define your boundaries and set your relational standards, you need to communicate them — clearly and simply — and then stand by them. Consider again the examples from the group discussion portion of this session:

I'm not participating.

I'm not going there with you.

If the conversation goes toward complaining, trash talk, or gossip, I need to step away.

The next time you try to get me to do something I don't want to do, I'll leave the room.

That activity is not good for me. I need to take a pass.

What boundary statements do you need to communicate to the person whose name you circled on the list on pages 53 – 54?

What fears or concerns are you aware of when you think about communicating your boundaries to this person?

How do you hope things might change for you if you are able to communicate your boundaries to this person and to stand by them?

For additional guidance on boundaries, see *Boundaries: When to Say Yes, When to Say No, to Take Control of Your Life* by Henry Cloud and John Townsend. For detailed guidance on specific situations, you may also benefit from the authors' books on boundaries in dating, marriage, and with kids; as well as *Boundaries Face to Face: How to Have That Difficult Conversation You've Been Avoiding.*

● Guided Prayer

God, thank you for the people you've put in my life — even the ones who aren't so easy to love. I believe that you can use every relationship I have to help me grow.

The person I'm struggling with most right now is ... This relationship is hard on me because ...

The boundary I think I need to set in this relationship is ...

When I think about communicating this boundary, I feel a mix of emotions and concerns. I especially need your help with ...

Thank you, Lord, for helping me to understand more about what it means to honor you in all of my relationships. I trust you to give me the courage and strength I need to set my boundaries and stand by them. Amen.

SEPTIC THOUGHTS

Overcoming Our False Beliefs

Ruth
Work - praise
Kreg + Jenni

It is amazing how often people think they are the victim of whatever thoughts happen to be running through their heads. It is as if they are passive specta-tors watching thoughts run across the screen, with no control over what's on it. But there is a fundamental battle in the spiritual life being waged by the Evil One over the nature of the thoughts that run through your mind. The ultimate freedom that you have that no one can take away even in a concentration camp, is the freedom to decide what your mind will dwell on.

JOHN ORTBERG, *THE ME I WANT TO BE*

Group Discussion: Checking In (5 Minutes)

Welcome to Session 4 of *Soul Detox*. A key part of getting to know God better is sharing your journey with others. Before watching the video, briefly check in with each other about your experiences since the last session. For example:

- What insights did you discover in the personal study or in the chapter you read from the *Soul Detox* book?
- How did the last session impact your daily life or your relationship with God?
- What questions would you like to ask the other members of your group?

Video: Septic Thoughts (13 Minutes)

Play the video segment for Session 4. As you watch, use the outline (below and pages 61 – 63) to follow along or to take notes on anything that stands out to you.

Notes

"For as he thinks in his heart, so is he" (Proverbs 23:7a NKJV).

The thought really does count, because what you think determines what you become.

"Carefully guard your thoughts because they are the source of true life" (Proverbs 4:23 CEV).

"We take captive every thought to make it obedient to Christ" (2 Corinthians 10:5b).

Four categories of toxic thoughts

1. Negative thoughts (pessimism)

2. Fearful thoughts (anxiety)

3. Discontented thoughts (bitterness)

4. Critical thoughts (criticism)

You will always find what you're looking for.

We must renew our thoughts.

"And the peace of God, which transcends all understanding, will guard your hearts and your minds in Christ Jesus" (Philippians 4:7).

"Finally, brothers and sisters, whatever is true, whatever is noble, whatever is right, whatever is pure, whatever is lovely, whatever is admirable — if anything is excellent or praiseworthy — think about such things" (Philippians 4:8).

Don't think about what you can't do; think about what God's Word says you can do.

WHEN YOU THINK ...	REPLACE IT WITH ...
I don't have what it takes.	I can do all things through Christ who gives me strength (Philippians 4:13).
I'm never going to get over this.	I am an overcomer by the blood of the Lamb and by the words of [my] testimony (Revelation 12:11).
I'm never going to have a great life.	God knew me before I was born; he has plans to bless me, to prosper me, and to use me (Psalm 139:16; Jeremiah 29:11).
I can't make a difference in this world.	God is working in all things to bring about good to those who love him and are called according to his purpose (Romans 8:28).

"Do not conform to the pattern of this world, but be transformed by the renewing of your mind" (Romans 12:2).

"The weapons we fight with are not the weapons of the world. On the contrary, they have divine power to demolish strongholds" (2 Corinthians 10:4).

"Yet you know me, LORD; you see me and test my thoughts about you. Drag them off like sheep to be butchered! Set them apart for the day of slaughter!" (Jeremiah 12:3).

Group Discussion (38 Minutes)

Take a few minutes to talk about what you just watched.

1. What part of the teaching had the most impact on you?

Distorted Thinking

2. What thoughts or emotions came to mind as you watched people writing their toxic thoughts on the walls at the beginning of the video?

3. Like toxic words, toxic thoughts distort the truth of who God made you to be. For example:

   I'll never overcome this issue/failure/addiction. Why try?
   I am loved because of my achievements. No achievements, no love.
   My security depends on having the right financial portfolio.

cont.

If I do everything perfectly from now on, I can make up for my past mistakes.

I hate myself. How could anyone else love me?

Everything in my life would be better if I were more attractive.

I could accomplish great things if only I had his money, her talents, or their smarts.

If I am careful and don't take any risks, nothing bad will happen to me and I will be happy.

- When you consider your struggles or insecurities, how would you describe the toxic thought(s) behind them?

- Briefly describe a recent situation that illustrates how this thought has impacted you (for example, your outlook, your behavior, your decisions, or how you relate to God and others).

Rogue Thoughts, Captive Thoughts

4. Just like a yellow traffic light is a sure indication that a red light is coming, our thoughts are a sure indication of where our lives are going. If our minds are dominated by rogue thoughts, our lives will become increasingly negative and disconnected from God. The apostle Paul uses strong language in describing how to address this concern:

   We demolish arguments and every pretension that sets itself up against the knowledge of God, and we take captive every thought to make it obedient to Christ (2 Corinthians 10:5).

For a fresh perspective on this verse, read it again from *The Message*:

> We use our powerful God-tools for smashing warped philosophies, tearing down barriers erected against the truth of God, fitting every loose thought and emotion and impulse into the structure of life shaped by Christ (2 Corinthians 10:5 MSG).

- For some, this familiar verse raises the discouraging prospect of "thought police" and previous failed efforts to "try really hard" *not* to think certain thoughts. How do the analogies — of taking thoughts captive, making them obedient, fitting them into a structure — challenge rather than reinforce this perspective?

- In practical terms, how would you describe what it means to fit loose thoughts into the structure of life shaped by Christ?

- Recall the toxic thought you identified in response to question 3 (pages 63–64). What thoughts or emotions are you aware of when you think about making this thought obedient to Christ?

Mind Makeover

5. The apostle Paul describes a supernatural antidote to the poison of toxic thoughts:

> Do not conform to the pattern of this world, but be transformed by the renewing of your mind (Romans 12:2a).

The Greek word translated as "renewing" is *anakainōsis* (an-ak-ah´-ee-no-sis), which means "to restore, to renovate, to make better than new." Paul uses this same word to describe the transformation that happens when we surrender our lives to Christ:

> He saved us through the washing of rebirth and *renewal* by the Holy Spirit, whom he poured out on us generously through Jesus Christ our Savior (Titus 3:5b – 6, emphasis added).

- Take a moment to recall your first *renewal* — the process and events that led to your salvation and the changes you experienced when you gave your life to Christ.* Briefly describe what stands out most to you about that experience.

- How might the renewal process you experienced in salvation help you to understand what it means to experience an ongoing renewal of your mind and thoughts now?

6. At this point, touch base with each other about how you're doing in the group. Use one of the sentence starters below, or your own statement, to help the group learn more about the best way to companion you.

I want to give you permission to challenge me more about …

An area where I really need your help or sensitivity is …

It always helps me to feel more connected to the group when …

Something I've learned about myself because of this group is …

---

* Those of us who come to faith as adults are often very clear about what led us to faith and the difference Christ has made in our lives. However, if you came to faith as a child, your process and transformation are no less significant. For this recollection, you might consider especially how God used your childlike faith or caring adults to draw you to Christ, and the relationships and experiences that have been most significant in your spiritual growth.

Individual Activity: What I Want to Remember (2 Minutes)

1. Briefly review the outline and any notes you took.

2. In the space below, write down the most significant thing you gained in this session — from the teaching, activities, or discussions.

What I want to remember from this session ...

Stepanie's son Josh

Election

Cam Whitehead

Larry - Colonoscopy

Closing Prayer

Close your time together with prayer.

GET A HEAD START ON THE DISCUSSION FOR SESSION 5

As part of the group discussion for Session 5, you'll have an opportunity to talk about what you've learned and experienced together throughout the *Soul Detox* curriculum. Between now and your next meeting, consider taking a few moments to review the previous sessions and identify the teaching, discussions, or activities that stand out most to you. Use the worksheet on pages 68–69 to briefly summarize the highlights of what you've learned and experienced.

Session 5 Head Start Worksheet

Take a few moments to reflect on what you've learned and experienced throughout the *Soul Detox* curriculum. You may want to review notes from the DVD teaching, what you wrote down for "What I Want to Remember" at the end of each group session, responses in the personal studies, etc. Here are some questions you might consider as part of your review:

- What struggles or progress did I experience related to this session?

- What was the most important thing I learned about myself in this session?

- How did I experience God's presence or leading related to this session?

- How did this session impact my relationships with the other people in the group?

Use the spaces provided below and on the next page to briefly summarize what you've learned and experienced for each session.

Session 1 Lethal Language: Experiencing the Power of Life-Giving Words (pages 9–29)

Scare Pollution: Unlocking the Chokehold of Fear (pages 31–44)

 Radioactive Relationships: Loving Unhealthy People without Getting Sick (pages 45–58)

 Septic Thoughts: Overcoming Our False Beliefs (pages 59–77)

Personal Study

● Read and Learn

Read chapter 2 of the *Soul Detox* book. Use the space below to note any insights or questions you want to bring to the next group session.

● Study and Reflect

The root of most sins we commit outwardly is the false beliefs we embrace inwardly. In order to experience a life of purity with a clean heart, we must identify and reject the toxic thoughts that keep us from God's best. We don't need Dr. Phil to tell us what God revealed to us in his Word thousands of years ago: your thoughts determine who you become (Proverbs 23:7).

Soul Detox, page 38

1. In the course of a typical week, what areas of your life tend to routinely generate negative thoughts? Check all that apply:

☐ My past
☐ My future
☐ My relationships
☐ My job or daily responsibilities
☐ My to-do list
☐ My finances

☐ My health
☐ My gifts/skills/abilities
☐ My appearance
☐ My spiritual life
☐ My life in general
☐ Other:

Of the items you checked, which stand out as those you struggle with most? Circle the top two or three.

Next, write the items you circled from the list in the left column of the chart on page 71. Use the right column to write down some of the toxic thoughts you have in that area of your life. (See question 3 on pages 63–64 to review some examples of toxic thoughts.)

AREAS OF MY LIFE	MY TOXIC THOUGHTS

Briefly review the toxic thoughts you wrote down on the chart. Circle the one that seems most entrenched or most difficult for you right now.

How has this particular false belief led to personal failure in your past? For example, a false belief such as, "I am loved only when I achieve," may have led a student to cheat on a class assignment for a better grade. "I am only secure if I have enough money" might have led a person to lie about income to avoid paying higher taxes.

How might this false belief make you vulnerable to personal failure now?

Where is this particular false belief leading you in the future? In other words, what kind of person could you become if this toxic thought continues unchallenged?

When you think God thoughts, he will guard your mind with peace. Instead of meditating on poison, you will meditate on truth. You might not see an overnight change in your life, but if you direct your thoughts toward God, I promise you that over time your life will be more joyful and peace-filled.

Soul Detox, pages 45–46

---

2. In his letter to the church at Philippi, the apostle Paul describes a process for moving from a mind harassed by toxic thoughts to a mind guarded by God's peace:

> Don't worry about anything; instead, pray about everything. Tell God what you need, and thank him for all he has done. Then you will experience God's peace, which exceeds anything we can understand. His peace will guard your hearts and minds as you live in Christ Jesus (Philippians 4:6 – 7 NLT).

Paul teaches a simple, two-part prayer that leads to peace: (1) tell God what you need, and (2) thank him for all he has done. What do you need from God in connection with the toxic thought you circled on the chart on page 71?

What has God already done that you can thank him for?

3. Paul goes on to provide additional instructions for keeping our minds at peace:

> Fix your thoughts on what is *true*, and *honorable*, and *right*, and *pure*, and *lovely*, and *admirable*. Think about things that are *excellent* and *worthy of praise*. Keep putting into practice all you learned and received from me — everything you heard from me and saw me doing. Then the God of peace will be with you (Philippians 4:8 – 9 NLT, emphasis added).

The left column of the chart on pages 74 – 75 includes the eight emphasized words and phrases from the Philippians passage. As you reflect on the meaning of these words, use the right column to write down any connections you make between the words and the toxic thought you circled on the chart on page 71. Connections could include exposing a lie you may have bought into, discovering a new perspective, making a confession, naming what you need from God, or anything else that comes to mind when you consider your toxic thought in light of the words on the chart.

I CAN FIX MY MIND ON WHAT IS …	HOW THIS WORD CONNECTS TO MY TOXIC THOUGHT
True: valid, reliable, honest, sincere, real, faithful, trustworthy	
Honorable: noble, worthy of reverence, holy	
Right: upright, just, worthy of God's approval	
Pure: holy, spotless, uncorrupted, whole	

I CAN FIX MY MIND ON WHAT IS ...	HOW THIS WORD CONNECTS TO MY TOXIC THOUGHT
Lovely: pleasing, agreeable, pleasant, graceful	
Admirable: praiseworthy, attractive, meeting the highest standards	
Excellent: virtuous, good and correct behavior, exhibiting qualities that make up good character	
Worthy of praise: highly regarded, commendable, laudable, exemplary	

Please don't limit [yourself] to self-affirmations and positive thinking. I'm not saying you shape your life with good thoughts. I'm saying you shape it with God thoughts.

Soul Detox, page 49

4. Briefly review the connections you wrote on your chart (pages 74 – 75). Use the truths you identified to write one or two "God thoughts" you can use to capture your toxic thought and "make it obedient to Christ" (2 Corinthians 10:5).

● Guided Prayer

God, thank you for the promise that your peace will guard my heart and my mind.

Sometimes my thoughts run in crazy directions or get fixated on something I wish I could let go of. Right now, the thoughts I'm struggling with are …

What I need from you is …

Thank you for all that you have already done for me, especially for …

Lord, I want to fix my mind on you. Please take my thoughts captive and make them obedient to you — today and every day. Amen.

GERM WARFARE

Cleansing Our Lives of Cultural Toxins

In America, it is hard to distinguish Christianity from
its social and cultural setting. It blends into the scenery.

THOMAS C. ODEN, *THE CHRISTIAN ADVOCATE*

Beth Kennedy family
Pray for our country

Group Discussion: Checking In (5 Minutes)

Welcome to Session 5 of *Soul Detox*. A key part of getting to know God better is sharing your journey with others. Before watching the video, briefly check in with each other about your experiences since the last session. For example:

- What insights did you discover in the personal study or in the chapter you read from the *Soul Detox* book?
- How did the last session impact your daily life or your relationship with God?
- What questions would you like to ask the other members of your group?

Video: Germ Warfare (12 Minutes)

Play the video segment for Session 5. As you watch, use the outline (below and pages 81 – 82) to follow along or to take notes on anything that stands out to you.

Notes

Cultural toxins are things that may be culturally acceptable but actually hurt our souls.

"Like a muddied spring or a polluted well is a righteous man who gives way to the wicked" (Proverbs 25:26 NIV 1984).

We need to take an inventory of what we consume from culture — books, articles, websites, games, music, movies, friends, etc.

Just because something is common behavior doesn't make it right.

"Don't become so well-adjusted to your culture that you fit into it without even thinking. Instead, fix your attention on God. You'll be changed from the inside out. Readily recognize what he wants from you, and quickly respond to it. Unlike the culture around you, always dragging you down to its level of immaturity, God brings the best out of you, develops well-formed maturity in you" (Romans 12:2 MSG).

Is culture bringing out the best in me or is it dragging me down to a lower level of maturity?

A caution: We must fight against the temptation to become legalistic in this process.

Just because we could — do something, watch something, see something, go somewhere — doesn't mean we should.

" 'Everything is permissible for me' — but not everything is beneficial. 'Everything is permissible for me' — but I will not be mastered by anything" (1 Corinthians 6:12 NIV 1984).

How do we know what is beneficial, helpful and acceptable in all the things we consume?

"Test everything. Hold on to the good. Avoid every kind of evil" (1 Thessalonians 5:21 – 22 NIV 1984).

Test everything by asking two questions:

1. Am I being entertained by sin?

2. Does this draw me closer to God or does it draw me away from God?

Our perception of what's pleasing to God could be very different from what actually is pleasing to God.

God's Word is our "white balance."

Group Discussion (39 Minutes)

Take a few minutes to talk about what you just watched.

1. What part of the teaching had the most impact on you?

Cultural Consumption

2. Recall a few of your cultural choices over the last week or two. Consider the media you consumed, such as magazines, websites, books, movies, television shows, social media, games, apps, music, performances, etc.

   Using your media choices as a reference point, how would you describe the dominant messages of your culture? Specifically, consider what the things you have read, watched, listened to, or experienced have communicated about at least three to five of the areas of life listed in the following chart.

ON THE TOPIC OF ...	THE DOMINANT MESSAGE OF MY CULTURE IS ...
Example: **Money**	*Get all you can and spend all you can.*
Money	
How to handle conflict	
Marriage	
Happiness	
Sex	
Success	
Appearance/beauty	
Work	

How would you describe the impact these cultural messages have on you?

3. Following are three definitions of "culture." Go around the group and have a different person read each definition aloud. As the definitions are read, underline any words or phrases that stand out to you. You may wish to read through the list twice to give everyone time to listen and respond.

> The artistic and social pursuits, expression, and tastes valued by a society or class, including the arts, manners, dress, etc.

> The attitudes, feelings, values, and behavior that characterize and inform society as a whole or any social group within it.

> The totality of socially transmitted behavior patterns, arts, beliefs, institutions, and all other products of human work and thought. Culture is learned and shared within social groups and is transmitted socially.

• What words or phrases stood out to you? Why?

• *Culture is a system of beliefs and values. Participating in a culture constitutes agreement with and promotion of its beliefs and values.* Do you agree or disagree with these statements? In what cases, if any, would you make an exception to your position? Share the reasons for your response.

Banquet 32
Pam Whitehead
Joan Rotti

Cultural Adjustment

4. In a familiar passage from Romans, the apostle Paul acknowledges the stunting influence that following cultural norms can have on our ability to know and follow God:

> Do not conform any longer to the pattern of this world, but be transformed by the renewing of your mind. Then you will be able to test and approve what God's will is — his good, pleasing and perfect will (Romans 12:2).

On the DVD, Craig read this same passage from *The Message*:

> Don't become so well-adjusted to your culture that you fit into it without even thinking. Instead, fix your attention on God. You'll be changed from the inside out. Readily recognize what he wants from you, and quickly respond to it. Unlike the culture around you, always dragging you down to its level of immaturity, God brings the best out of you, develops well-formed maturity in you (Romans 12:2 MSG).

- To what degree would you say that your cultural choices — about the media you consume, clothes you wear, language you use, etc. — are ones you make without even thinking? Choose a number on the continuum below and briefly describe your response.

1	2	3	4	5
To a minimal degree I am very aware of and intentional about all of my cultural choices.		**To a moderate degree** I am occasionally aware of and intentional about some of my cultural choices.		**To a great degree** I am rarely aware of or intentional about any of my cultural choices.

- Now identify an area in which you are having a hard time spiritually (for example, an inability to trust God with a problem, trouble connecting with God in prayer, difficulty establishing a regular practice of spiritual disciplines, a struggle with temptation, etc.). Briefly name your struggle for the group and then discuss together the questions on page 86.

(1) *What are the dominant messages your culture might give you about this issue?* For example, "If you're busy, you're important," might be a cultural message for someone who struggles to make time for a regular practice of prayer. Or "You only live once!" might be a cultural message for someone who struggles with a temptation. (As a reference, you may wish to recall some of your responses to question 2, page 84.)

(2) *How might these cultural messages complicate your struggle, or make it difficult for you to allow God to use your struggle to bring out the best in you?*

Test Everything

5. When it comes to making decisions about what is beneficial and acceptable, the biblical wisdom is, "Test everything" (1 Thessalonians 5:21 – 22). On the DVD, Craig said he tests his cultural choices by asking two questions:

   Am I being entertained by sin?

   Does this draw me closer to God or does it draw me away from God?

   • When you think about your cultural choices over the last day or two, which pass the two-question test? Which fail?

- Do you think it's possible for the answer to the second question to be "neither"? In other words, is it possible for some things to be neutral, having neither a positive nor negative impact on spiritual growth and maturity? Why or why not?

Wrap-Up

6. Discuss what you've learned and experienced together throughout the *Soul Detox* curriculum.

- What would you say is the most important thing you learned? How has it impacted you (for example, in your attitudes, behaviors, relationships, etc.)?

- How have you recognized God at work in your life through the study? What do you sense God's invitation to you might be?

- At the end of every session, you had an opportunity to talk about what you needed from the other members of the group and how you could be good companions for one another. What changes, if any, have you noticed in the ways you interact with each other now compared to the beginning of the curriculum?

Individual Activity: What I Want to Remember (2 Minutes)

1. Briefly review the outline and any notes you took.
2. In the space below, write down the most significant thing you gained in this session — from the teaching, activities, or discussions.

   What I want to remember from this session ...

Closing Prayer

Close your time together with prayer.

Personal Study

● Read and Learn

Read chapter 10 of the *Soul Detox* book. Use the space below to note any insights or questions you want to bring to the next group session.

● Study and Reflect

It's a good idea every now and then to take an inventory of the things that you consume from culture.

Craig Groeschel, *Soul Detox* DVD

1. Use the chart on pages 90 – 91 to take a brief inventory of your cultural consumption. For each category, use the center column to list two to four examples of things you routinely or recently consumed. Be as specific as possible. For example, in music, list song titles, not just a music style or genre.

   In the right column on the chart, do a quick assessment of what you consume. Use the following symbols:

   > ↑ = Includes or promotes content that is *consistent* with my values and with biblical teaching
   >
   > ↓ = Includes or promotes content that is *inconsistent* with my values and with biblical teaching
   >
   > — = Content is *neutral*, neither consistent nor inconsistent with my values and biblical teaching

   For your assessments, try to choose either an up or a down arrow. If an item has a mix of content, you can use both an up and a down arrow. Some items may seem neutral (—) but could also be ↑ or ↓ depending on your use. For example, a social media website might seem neutral but could be ↑ if you use it to stay connected to people you care about, or ↓ if it routinely causes you to neglect other important aspects of your life.

CULTURE CATEGORY	WHAT I CONSUME	▲ ▼ —
Example: **Internet-based media** (websites, blogs, podcasts, etc.)	*FAIL Blog* *Pray-as-You-Go podcast* *DoItYourself.com* *Huffington Post*	▼ ▲ — ▼ ▲
Social Media		
Internet-based media (websites, blogs, podcasts, etc.)		
Apps		
Games		
Music		
Movies		

CULTURE CATEGORY	WHAT I CONSUME	▲ ▼ —
Television		
Radio		
Events (concerts, performances, sports, etc.)		
Clubs or restaurants		
Books		
Magazines		
Other:		

Briefly review your culture inventory and your assessments. What stands out most to you?

Circle one or two of the things you assessed with a ⬇. What images, language, stories, or experiences does it include that contradict your values or biblical teaching?

It's tempting to think that what we watch on TV, see at the movies, listen to on our iPods, play on our gaming systems, and read before bedtime doesn't affect us. But it does.... We must take the images, language, and stories we allow into our minds and hearts very seriously. We must disinfect our hearts with the germ-killing power of the truth.

Soul Detox, page 178

---

2. On the DVD, Craig told a story about a mom who put a teaspoon of dog poop in her son's favorite brownies to make a point. Her son had asked to watch a movie he said had "only a little bit of bad stuff in it." When he found out about the poop, her son was disgusted and refused to eat the brownies, but the mom said, "Don't worry, buddy. I didn't put a lot of poop in the brownies. There's just a little bit of bad stuff." The moral of the story? A little bit of poop goes a long way.

   What is your initial reaction to this story in terms of how it might apply to the items you assessed with a ⬇ on your chart (pages 90 – 91)?

Of the items you assessed with a ↓, which one would be the hardest for you to step away from? Why?

"Everything is permissible for me," was both a common saying and a dominant cultural influence that caused problems for the early Christians in Corinth. In his first letter to the Corinthians, the apostle Paul affirms the truth that all things are permissible, but he also goes on to state two deeper truths: "not everything is beneficial," and "I will not be mastered by anything" (1 Corinthians 6:12 NIV 1984).

Following are three versions of 1 Corinthians 6:12. Read through the verses slowly and underline any words or phrases that stand out to you.

> Some of you say, "We can do anything we want to." But I tell you that not everything is good for us. So I refuse to let anything have power over me (CEV).

> Just because something is technically legal doesn't mean that it's spiritually appropriate. If I went around doing whatever I thought I could get by with, I'd be a slave to my whims (MSG).

> You say, "I am allowed to do anything" — but not everything is good for you. And even though "I am allowed to do anything," I must not become a slave to anything (NLT).

Of the words and phrases that stood out to you, which one seems to resonate most with you? Why?

How would you assess the item you identified at the top of page 93 that would be the hardest for you to step away from? Place an X on the continuum below to indicate your response.

●━━━━━━━━━━━━━━━━━━━━━━━━━━━━━━━━━●

Technically legal   **Spiritually appropriate**

How do you respond to the idea that this item could represent an area in which you might be a slave to your whims?

3. It's hard to think about potentially stepping away from things we enjoy, but the Bible affirms that nothing we give up is wasted — every surrender is an investment that yields long-term spiritual rewards.

> Don't become so well-adjusted to your culture that you fit into it without even thinking. Instead, fix your attention on God. *You'll be changed from the inside out.* Readily recognize what he wants from you, and quickly respond to it. Unlike the culture around you, always dragging you down to its level of immaturity, *God brings the best out of you, develops well-formed maturity in you* (Romans 12:2 MSG, emphasis added).

If you sense God may be inviting you to let go of something, how do you hope he might use your surrender to change you from the inside out, bring the best out of you, or develop maturity in you?

● Guided Prayer

God, thank you for all the richness and diversity of the culture I live in. There are so many good things I can enjoy.

It's not always easy for me to recognize the toxic impact of the cultural things I consume. Please increase my awareness and help me to be more intentional about my choices. I want to be more sensitive especially with what I consume in these areas ...

I ask for wisdom to distinguish what is permissible from what is spiritually appropriate. Right now, I believe you may be asking me to step away from ... because ...

I have friends who may be confused or upset if I step away from something we've enjoyed doing together. I ask for your help especially in my relationship with ...

Lord, I want to want you more than I want anything else. Give me a strong heart to live radically committed to you, and a surrendered heart to let go of anything that could keep me from growing closer to you. Amen.

Share Your Thoughts

With the Author: Your comments will be forwarded to the author when you send them to *zauthor@zondervan.com*.

With Zondervan: Submit your review of this book by writing to *zreview@zondervan.com*.

Free Online Resources at
www.zondervan.com

Zondervan AuthorTracker: Be notified whenever your favorite authors publish new books, go on tour, or post an update about what's happening in their lives at www.zondervan.com/authortracker.

Daily Bible Verses and Devotions: Enrich your life with daily Bible verses or devotions that help you start every morning focused on God. Visit www.zondervan.com/newsletters.

Free Email Publications: Sign up for newsletters on Christian living, academic resources, church ministry, fiction, children's resources, and more. Visit www.zondervan.com/newsletters.

Zondervan Bible Search: Find and compare Bible passages in a variety of translations at www.zondervanbiblesearch.com.

Other Benefits: Register yourself to receive online benefits like coupons and special offers, or to participate in research.

ZONDERVAN®

ZONDERVAN.com/
AUTHORTRACKER
follow your favorite authors